Kai Tak
THE FINAL DECADE

Kai Tak
THE FINAL DECADE

Robbie Shaw

Airlife
England

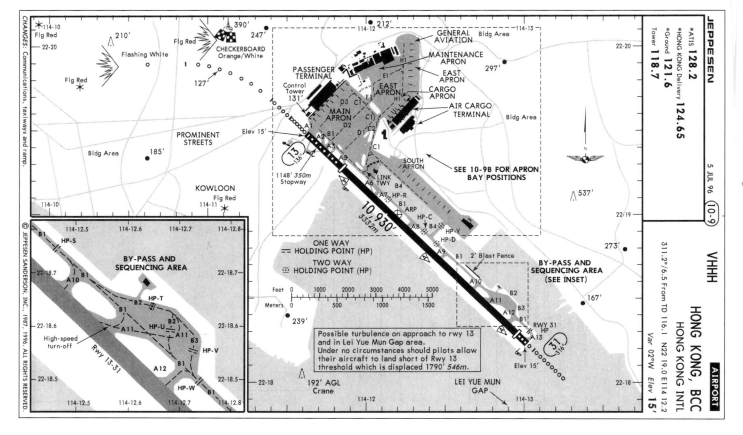

FRONT COVER: A Cathay Pacific 747 fifteen seconds from touchdown on runway 13.

BACK COVER: Gates 1 and 2 seen at night in 1987.

Copyright© 1997 Robbie Shaw

First published in the UK in 1997
by Airlife Publishing Ltd

British Library Cataloguing in Publication Data
A catalogue record for this book
is available from the British Library

ISBN 1 85310 832 4

Typeset by Phoenix Typesetting, Ilkley, West Yorkshire.

Printed in Hong Kong

Airlife Publishing Ltd
101 Longden Road, Shrewsbury, SY3 9EB, England

Introduction

For many years now Hong Kong has been one of the world's major trading centres, which is evident by the large number of ships in Victoria Harbour and Kwai Chung container terminal. However, in the past decade the territory's international airport at Kai Tak has played an ever-increasing role in the movement of both passengers and freight. Both have shown phenomenal growth. In 1986 10.6 million passengers passed through the airport, a figure which by 1993 had risen to 24.5 million. That is slightly more than the number using London–Gatwick, and about half as many as London–Heathrow.

Kai Tak is almost at saturation point. The terminal building is closely surrounded by the concrete jungle of blocks of flats of Kowloon City, while the runway is built on reclaimed land extending into Kowloon Bay and Victoria Harbour. The ramp space has virtually doubled within the last ten years, due to further reclamation from the sea. A second cargo terminal has had to be built while the passenger terminal has seen limited expansion. It is physically impossible to expand the airport any further, so a replacement airport is currently being built at Chek Lap Kok on the northern shore of Lantau Island. This is the largest island among the 300-plus which comprise the territory of Hong Kong and, like Kai Tak, much of the airport is being constructed on reclaimed land.

Kai Tak has for some time been renowned as having one of the most difficult approaches of any airport in the world. This is not just due to the geographical location of its single runway 13/31, but also to the turbulence and wind shear from the adjacent hills, not to mention the intense heat reflected from the millions of tons of concrete in Kowloon City in the middle of the stiflingly hot summer. Approach paths to the runway are diverse to say the least: the approach to runway 31 is over the sea – straightforward ILS (Instrument Landing System) with a PAR (Precision Approach Radar) for back-up. After flying over the outer marker at Tathong Island, 5.7 miles from touchdown, the aeroplane passes through the Lei Yue Mun Gap which separates Hong Kong Island from the mainland on Kowloon side. On final approach the mast tops of ferries passing underneath can appear unnervingly close.

The approach to runway 13, however, has to be one of the most interesting and exciting in the world. Due to the mountainous terrain, a straight-in approach on the runway heading of 135° is not possible, therefore an offset approach is necessary using the IGS (Instrument Guidance System) which is based on ILS. After crossing the western part of crowded Victoria Harbour, aircraft 'coast in' over the crowded Kowloon districts of Sham Shui Po and Mong Kok on a heading of 088°. On approaching the middle marker at 1.8 miles from touchdown, pilots must take over visually and execute a 47° turn to align with the runway. It is quite something to watch a 747 making this manoeuvre – and even more so to experience it from within, as the towering buildings flash past seemingly inches from the wingtips. You are almost close enough to see what people are having for their evening meal in their living rooms! (Those of a nervous disposition are recommended *not* to look out of the windows at this stage of the flight.) If for any reason the pilot is unable to acquire the runway visually then he must immediately commence the missed approach procedure. To help him visually, the hillside beyond the middle marker is painted in huge red and white squares and is known as the 'Checkerboard'. Obviously, runway 31 departures have to make a sharp left turn soon after take-off, while in poor weather runway 13 departures are radar-monitored until the aircraft passes safely through the Lei Yue Mun Gap. On more than one occasion I have heard a controller urgently warn a departing aircraft to alter course as it has drifted towards the hills on either side of the Gap.

For noise abatement reasons the airport is closed at night, and for similar reasons late-evening and sometimes early-morning movements can suffer slight delays. This is due to the preference at those times, subject to ambient wind conditions, for both arrivals and departures to be routed over the sea; departures on 13 and arrivals on 31.

In the last few years there has been a tremendous increase in the number of aircraft enthusiasts and photographers from all over the world visiting Kai Tak. Most are from Europe, particularly the UK, Germany, Holland and Switzerland, as well as the occasional Australian or

American. Some now make it an annual pilgrimage. The reasons are various. They have seen in magazines or from friends the stunning photographs which can be taken, and with the impending closure of Kai Tak time is running out, and of course in real terms the cost of long-distance travel has fallen considerably.

My first visit to Hong Kong was in 1983 to visit friends working there, and, although I was only interested in military photography in those days, I did take a few shots of airliners. Little did I realise then that I was soon to spend two years there from 1986 to 1988 based at Sek Kong with the Royal Air Force. It was then that I decided I should record the CAAC Tridents on film for posterity, and I suddenly realised, 'Hey these airliners are really quite colourful'. (During this period everything in Europe from A-10s to C-5s was being painted 'grot' green.) Since then I have been an avid airliner photographer. I have had the opportunity twice in recent years to renew my acquaintance with Kai Tak, and although traffic is a little busier, it is the number of Jumbos, particularly freighters, which now operate into the airport that surprised me. From a photographer's point of view the big plus is the number of Chinese airlines serving the airport, a far cry from the rather staid CAAC livery.

The air traffic controllers at Kai Tak now handle about thirty-six runway movements an hour which, considering almost all movements are by aircraft in the 'heavy' vortex wake category, is commendable. It's not as high as the fifty-plus an hour regularly handled by Gatwick's single runway where they have a lot of smaller aircraft as well, but it is certainly far higher than the twenty-four an hour handled by Tokyo's Narita Airport.

Chek Lap Kok was originally planned to open in the spring of 1997, just before the handover of Hong Kong to the People's Republic of China. This projected date has now slipped to April 1998. There has been much discussion as well as pressure from airlines, because when Chek Lap Kok opens its single runway it will be close to full capacity from day one, despite the fact it will be a twenty-four hour airport; this pressure has been successful as it has recently been announced that a second runway is now to be built, although it will not be available in time for the airport's opening.

Although there are no spectator facilities at Kai Tak, enthusiasts have found many places where excellent photographs can be taken. There are unlikely to be any spectator facilities at Chek Lap Kok either, and I'm certain the quality of photographs available from outside the airport will not compare with those dramatic shots taken by many from the vantage points around Kai Tak. Unfortunately no help or assistance was forthcoming from the Kai Tak authorities in the preparation of this publication, though I must thank colleague Phil Parker for his assistance and filling in some gaps in my photographic coverage.

This book has been compiled by an enthusiast for the enthusiast, and for many I hope it will be a pleasant reminder and a memento of a visit to what is, and soon to be 'was', one of the most interesting international airports in the world.

Robbie Shaw

An aerial view of Kai Tak in 1987. Note how the runway extends into Victoria Harbour and is surrounded on three sides by water, while the terminal building and ramp have buildings encroaching right up to the airport boundary fence.

Hong Kong Is Home

For the last few decades civil aviation in Hong Kong was Cathay Pacific. The airline has for some time been one of the most successful in Asia, and continues to be so. The airline's fleet continues to expand at a steady rate, particularly its long-haul Boeing 747 fleet. Its large fleet of Lockheed L-1011 TriStars are well on the way to obsolescence, being replaced by the highly successful and fuel-efficient Airbus A330s and A340s. As these words are written the airline is poised to receive the first of its latest purchase, the Boeing 777. Indirect competition to Cathay came in the shape of Dragonair in 1986. Despite having only a small fleet of Boeing 737s on a few charter routes, Cathay was not impressed when the fledgling carrier was given additional routes. Ultimately both airlines formed a working relationship, with Cathay taking thirty per cent of the Swire Group holding in Dragonair. Further co-operation saw Cathay seconding personnel, including a few aircrew, to operate a pair of TriStars leased to the smaller carrier. Eventually Cathay pulled out of mainland China completely as it felt Dragonair could serve this market better, though Cathay, of course, fed a lot of intercontinental traffic on to these routes.

On the cargo side, Air Hong Kong operates a small fleet of 747 freighters, having disposed of the 707s previously operated. Transcorp operated a 707 freighter service to Australia but did not last very long. Formed in 1978, Heliservices is still going strong in the helicopter ad hoc charter market, operating the Lama and Ecureuil. Although based at Sek Kong in the New Territories its helicopters are a frequent sight around the skies of Kai Tak, Kowloon and Hong Kong Island, hence their inclusion.

For many years the Lockheed L-1011 TriStar was the backbone of Cathay Pacific's fleet used on regional Asian routes. Now that Airbus A330s and A340s are being delivered the TriStars are in the process of being disposed of. The first few aircraft were leased from Eastern Airlines, and for a time still wore their US registrations. With Lion Rock dominating the background L-1011-1 N316EA is towed on to the ramp from the HAECO maintenance hangars

Captured on film with the 'Dunlops' poised to impact the concrete of runway 13 is L-1011 Super TriStar 1 VR-HHW. This aircraft formerly served with Court Line as G-BAAB. Sister ship 'AA was also acquired by Cathay when Court Line ceased operations.

During the 1980s Cathay's long-range routes were the domain of its fleet of Boeing 747s, the first of which was 747-267B VR-HIA. This aircraft was the second Jumbo to be delivered to Cathay and was photographed in May 1986. The stretch of water in the background just above the tail of the 747 was known as 'the nullah', a most noxious stretch of water, most of which has since been filled in to make way for more ramp space.

Left:
A Cathay 747 over the rooftops of Kowloon some fifteen seconds from touchdown on runway 13. Despite the approach to the runway being over one of the most crowded areas on earth there has never been a serious fatal incident, thankfully.

Below:
Due to the constricted area upon which the airport has been built there is insufficient room for enough airbridges, therefore most aircraft are turned round on the spacious ramp. Some final maintenance work is being carried out on this Cathay 747 before a late-evening departure for Europe.

Cathay Boeing 747-400 VR-HOP taxies to the ramp after landing on runway 13. Victoria Peak on Hong Kong Island is visible in the background. With the impending handover of the territory to the People's Republic of China Cathay has dispensed with the Union Jack on the fin of its aircraft.

In the autumn of 1994 Cathay Pacific unveiled a new livery featuring a 'brushstroke' logo on the fin. The first Jumbo to appear in the new livery was series -400 VR-HOT in November 1994, and it is seen taxying to its gate soon afterwards. Visible in the background just above the cockpit is the famous 'checker-board hill' where aircraft have to execute a 47° turn on to final approach for runway 13.

Three of the four types currently in Cathay's fleet are visible in this photograph. An Airbus A330 lines up on runway 13 with a 747 and L-1011 at the holding point awaiting their turn.

With thrust reversers still deployed A340-200 VR-HMS decelerates on roll-out from landing on runway 13. The mass of high-rise buildings dominating the background are on Hong Kong Island across the waters of Victoria Harbour.

Right:
Dragonair was formed in 1987 as a regional charter operator with a single Boeing 737. It has since grown into a successful scheduled carrier with a network of regional routes and a fleet currently comprising seven Airbus A320s and three A330s. With the Airbus aircraft came a new livery which, when compared to the original, is somewhat boring to say the least. Distinctive Lion Rock poses above the titling on this A320.

Below:
Dragonair's original bright orange scheme stands proud against the rare clear blue skies. Photographed in January 1987 Boeing 737-200 carries the registration VR-HYK, in honour of major investor, the late Sir Y.K. Pao.

One of seven A320s in use, VR-HYU taxies for an early-morning departure to Haikou in November 1994. Again, Lion Rock surveys all.

Sleek-looking A330-300 VR-HYB lines up on runway 13 with a Cathay 747-200 at the holding point.

Until the acquisition of the A330s Dragonair utilised a pair of leased Cathay Pacific TriStars on the high-density Beijing and Shanghai routes.

In 1987 a new freight operator Transcorp was formed with a single Boeing 707 aimed primarily at serving Australia. However, the aircraft concerned, VR-HTC named *Hong Kong Kowloon Trader,* seemed to spend much of its time on the ground rather than in the air, and the airline eventually ceased operations.

Air Hong Kong has graduated from being a 707 operator to one with three 747 freighters. There is much speculation at the moment that Cathay Pacific will transfer its 747 freighters to Air Hong Kong to operate on its behalf. Seen on final approach to runway 13 is ageing 747-132F VR-HKN, now in its twenty-sixth year of service.

Although not Kai Tak-based, Heliservices machines are regularly seen around the skies of Kowloon and Hong Kong Island. Based at the military helicopter base at Sek Kong the company operates Aérospatiale Lama and Ecureuil helicopters. In January 1988 Heliservices fleet comprised just two machines-: Lama VR-HIP and Ecureuil VR-HJD, both of which are illustrated here.

Chinese Connection

Direct flights between Taiwan and the People's Republic of China are prohibited, therefore Hong Kong, just ninety minutes' flying time from Taiwan, benefits immensely as a transit point. The numerous flights between Kai Tak and Taipei comprise not just those of China Airlines and Cathay Pacific but also of a number of other Asian carriers such as Thai International and Korean Air. Over the years an ever-increasing number of mainland China destinations have been added to Kai Tak's schedules. Since the dissolution of CAAC, China has seen numerous new airlines and colours take the place of CAAC's rather staid livery and awful standard of service. In the CAAC days, Tridents dominated the bulk of services as the

Hong Kong Civil Aviation Department would not permit Soviet- or Chinese-built aircraft to operate into the territory. These days the Tridents are long gone, replaced by Boeings, Boeings and more Boeings, with the occasional Airbus or McDonnell Douglas product thrown in for good measure.

In the 1980s Taiwan's China Airlines acquired both the Boeing 767-200 and Airbus A300 for use on regional routes. Only two of the former were acquired, and were eventually disposed of in favour of more A300s. Boeing 767-200 B-1836 was photographed from the Hong Kong Aviation Club compound while on final approach to runway 13 in October 1987.

Left:
A Kowloon resident's view of a China Airlines A300B4 inbound to runway 13. The Taiwanese national carrier operates a variety of types into Kai Tak, ranging from the A320 to Boeing 747-400s.

Below:
China Airlines took delivery of four MD-11s, though these are progressively being transferred to subsidiary Mandarin Airlines. Taxying on to runway 13 is B-153, the last of the four to be delivered.

China Airlines has so many flights between Taipei and Hong Kong that it is not uncommon to find two of the Taiwanese carrier's aircraft on the ground at the same time – in this case a pair of Boeing 747-400s.

China Airlines Boeing 747-400 3B-SMC on final approach to runway 13 with a background comprising towering high-rise flats and Lion Rock. This particular aircraft is on lease replacing a 747-400 B-165 which was a total loss after going off the end of Kai Tak's runway 13 into Victoria Harbour on 4 November 1993, barely five months after it had been delivered. Fortunately there was no loss of life on this occasion.

The Taiwanese carrier also operates numerous cargo flights between the two cities. These are operated by dedicated Boeing 747-200 freighters, such as B-198 seen here on roll-out after landing on runway 31.

China Airlines is in the process of transferring all four of its MD-11 tri-jets to subsidiary Mandarin Airlines. Mandarin aircraft can be seen at Kai Tak almost on a daily basis undertaking flights for its parent company, usually with Boeing 747SP aircraft like N4508H.

Right:
For many years the BAe (Hawker Siddeley) Trident was a regular sight at Kai Tak, operating the bulk of CAAC flights between the territory and mainland China. Residents living in the vicinity of the airport will tell you they were one of the noisiest types to have served the airport! Seen on a rather quiet Kai Tak ramp on a Saturday afternoon in April 1986 is Trident 2E B-2219.

Below:
Nostalgia! The sight and sound of the Trident at Kai Tak, alas, are no more. A few are still believed to be operational with China United Airlines, the commercial division of the Chinese Air Force. Illustrated is Trident 2E B-2217 in the colours of CAAC.

CAAC was also the last to operate the Boeing 707 on scheduled passenger services into Kai Tak.

CAAC soon became one of Boeing's best customers, and at one time its fleet comprised examples of the 707, 737, 747, 747SP, 757 and 767. The 727 was the only type Boeing's salesmen failed to convince the Chinese carrier to purchase, perhaps testimony to the Trident's qualities. Boeing 747SP B-2442 taxies to the holding point for runway 13 with a company 737 parked in the background.

Left:
Looking pristine in the afternoon sunshine is CAAC Boeing 747-200B B-2448. Like many of the fleet this aircraft was transferred to Air China when CAAC was dissolved as an airline.

Below:
CAAC no longer operates as an airline, but remains the regulatory body for aviation in the People's Republic of China. This situation has seen an explosion of new carriers serving every corner of this giant land mass. Air China is now classed as the official state airline and, with the exception of a new tail logo, its livery is identical to that once worn by CAAC aircraft. The Air China fleet is dominated by Boeings, with 737-300 B-2535 illustrated.

All of the former CAAC Boeing 747s were transferred to Air China, though the carrier has since added a number of the more modern series 400 variants, including B-2445 seen here in a typical pose turning on to final approach to runway 13.

Shanghai-based China Eastern operates a
varied fleet from a number of different manufacturers. Turning on to the runway is Fokker
F100 B-2233, and parked on gate 1 in the
background is one of the company's MD-11s.

Above:
Supplementing the Fokkers on short- and medium-range routes are a large number of McDonnell Douglas MD-82s; B-2127 is illustrated banking on to final approach. This photograph was taken in November 1994, with the hills in the background their normal brown parched colour after a long, hot, humid summer.

Right:
Airbus A300-600Rs are used by China Eastern on regional Asian routes as well as the high-density Hong Kong–Shanghai route. Taxying to its gate past a crowded ramp and concrete jungle of high-rise flats is B-2320.

Although China Eastern utilises its five-strong MD-11 fleet on intercontinental routes to the US and Europe the type is still regularly seen at Kai Tak, usually at least twice a day. Seen at the commencement of its take-off run from runway 13 is MD-11 B-2173. Note the Japan Airlines DC-10 in the background.

Above:
Another Chinese MD-82 operator is Shenyang-based China Northern Airlines. This airline operates just one or two flights a day, usually in the late afternoon. A number of the type previously served with CAAC, though this aircraft, B-2126, is one of a number assembled in China under licence.

Right:
Headquartered at Xian, China Northwest Airlines is another with a varied fleet, comprising An-24s, Y7s, BAe 146s, Tu-154s and Airbus A310s and A300s. Illustrated about to touchdown in the late afternoon is A310-200 B-2302. This aircraft is one of three operated, all of which are former CAAC machines.

China Southern Airlines is now one of the largest in China, comprising many Boeings as well as numerous commuter types. Based at Guangzhou (Canton) on the Pearl River delta the airline operates more services to Kai Tak than any other Chinese operator, and at times as many as five of the airline's aircraft can be seen on the ground at Kai Tak. Boeing 737s predominate in the airline's inventory, including the series 500 typified here by B-2547.

China Southern is also China's largest 757 operator, the first of which, B-2801, formerly served with CAAC. The airline also operates the 767 into Kai Tak, and has recently taken delivery of its first 777.

Above:
Chinese airlines tend to shy away from imaginative titles preferring to stick with regional identities. It is hardly surprising then that the airline serving the south-western province of Sichuan is China Southwest Airlines. This company's inventory is also predominantly Boeing-equipped with large numbers of 737s and 757s. Photographed about to land at Kai Tak on a flight from Chengdu, the capital of Sichuan Province, is Boeing 737-300 B-2522. This is yet another machine which was once a regular visitor to Kai Tak in CAAC guise.

Left:
The modest fleet of Xiamen Airlines consists of just two types, the Boeing 737 and 757. The latter type operates a daily service from its namesake city. The aircraft featured here, B-2829, has been in service with the airline since August 1993.

Around Asia

Air travel in Asia is booming. To cater for the massive increase in travel, many carriers are using larger aircraft; this is particularly true in Hong Kong where more and more flights are operated by 747 variants. Like Kai Tak, a number of the region's airports are already at, or near, full capacity and cannot accommodate an increased frequency of service. The continued need for more and more aircraft by the region's airlines is, of course, food and drink to the manufacturers' sales force, especially those of Airbus Industrie and Boeing. Airbus products, particularly the A300, made their mark very quickly among Asia's airlines. There is no doubt that the European manufacturer's successes in the area made an impact on Boeing, though the US company is still very dominant in the Chinese market. From the Airbus family the long-range A330 and A340 are now in service or on order by several of the region's airlines, while Thai, China Southern and Cathay have just taken delivery of their first Boeing 777 twin-jets. There is no doubt that for many years to come Asia is going to be an area of growth, and the main battleground for the sales forces of Airbus and Boeing.

Philippine Airlines has served Hong Kong for many years; it is only in recent years, however, that the airline introduced a direct service from Cebu. This service is operated by Boeing 737-300s, with RP-C4006 photographed at the start of its take-off roll.

Flights from the capital Manila to Hong Kong
are operated by both A300s and Boeing 747s,
the DC-10s which used to fly the route having
recently been sold. This photograph of
A300B4 RP-C3004 taken in 1986 gives the
opportunity to compare the livery with
the current one which was introduced in 1987.

Due to the high traffic density on the Manila–Hong Kong route Philippine Airlines' recently delivered Boeing 747-400s are frequently utilised on the service. (*Phil Parker*)

One of the more recently introduced services
is the BAe 146 freighter of Pacific East Asia
Cargo operated in partial TNT livery.

Right:
Asiana Airlines was founded in 1988 initially with Boeing 737-400 equipment. Its operations then were severely restricted: there were very few routes over which it was permitted to compete directly with Korean Air. These restrictions have now been lifted and the airline operates an expanding worldwide network. The airline's inventory is also expanding at a phenomenal rate, with a large number of Boeing 767s and 747-400s in use and on order. Both types are used on services to Hong Kong, with 747-400 HL7417 featured here.

Below:
Even in the late 1980s Korean Air still utilised Boeing 707s on services to Hong Kong, though only in a cargo capacity. This 1986 vintage shot shows HL7427 in the carrier's old livery.

Korean Air MD-11s were regularly used on the Seoul–Hong Kong route until 1995. However, now that the airline is converting its tri-jets to freighters this is no longer the case, though it's surely a matter of time before these aircraft supplement 747 freighters in their new role. Photographed in 1994 while still in passenger configuration is MD-11 HL7375.

Although Korean Air A300s can be seen in Kai Tak on an almost daily basis it is the airline's 747 Jumbos which dominate. Korean Air uses no fewer than five 747 variants on its Hong Kong services. These include the series 200, 200F, 300, 400 and the SP. Of the latter variant, HL7456 prepares for take-off from runway 13.

Wearing 'Visit Korea 94' promotional stickers
Boeing 747-300 HL7470 prepares for take-off,
bound for Seoul.

In recent years Vietnam Airlines has strived to enhance its image and efficiency. With assistance from Air France the airline leased a number of A320s and crews from the French carrier and set about expanding its ailing network. With the new equipment came approval to serve Hong Kong, which it does up to three times a day using both the A320s and leased Boeing 767s. Still wearing its French registration A320-200 F-GFKN is seen on its take-off roll with numerous 747s parked on the ramp behind.

Another carrier which only recently started flying to Hong Kong was Cambodia International Airlines. From Phnom-Penh the airline used a leased Boeing 737-200 which was later supplemented by a former Delta Air Lines Boeing 727-200. The former machine, N197AL, is seen about to land in November 1994 wearing a most colourful livery. Only a few months later the airline ceased operations.

Left:
From its humble beginnings Thai Airways International has emerged as one of the most successful Asian airlines. The airline continues to expand both its route network and fleet, so much so that no fewer than six different types are used on Hong Kong services, including the newly delivered Boeing 777. During the 1980s Airbus A300s operated the bulk of the airline's Kai Tak services.

Below:
Thai's DC-10s are seldom seen in Hong Kong skies these days; however McDonnell Douglas's latest tri-jet, the MD-11, is a frequent visitor, augmented by A330s and Boeing 747 variants. Seen turning on to final approach is MD-11 HS-TMG.

Thai currently operates the 200, 300 and 400 series of the 747, and all are regularly used on Hong Kong services. The older series 200 aircraft, like HS-TGS seen here, are soon to be disposed of as additional -400 variants are delivered.

Kai Tak is a Mecca for 747 freighters. Cargo has always played a vital role in the growth of Kai Tak, and the airport authorities have only just managed to keep pace with the tremendous growth. Nippon Cargo Airlines acquired its first 747 freighters in 1985 and the type has been a regular visitor ever since. This shot of Boeing 747-281F(SCD) JA8172 was taken in August 1987. Note that there are no fewer than six CAAC aircraft, including Tridents, Boeing 737s, an MD-80 and an A310 parked on the ramp behind.

For a number of years All Nippon Airways' Boeing 727s were sporadic visitors on charter flights; however in 1986 the airline finally received approval to operate a daily scheduled service to compete with Japan Airlines. This route was operated by Lockheed L-1011 TriStar 1 JA8521. Despite having a number of TriStars on its inventory only this aircraft had internal safety signs in English as well as Japanese.

All Nippon has since upgraded to Boeing 747 equipment on the Hong Kong route, with series 281B JA8190 illustrated on its take-off roll.

Of the foreign carriers Japan Air Lines is second only to China Airlines in the number of services operated through Kai Tak. Boeing 767s first appeared in 1986, these being the three series -200 aircraft acquired. However these were soon augmented by the larger -300 machines. Photographed in January 1988, only a few weeks after its delivery to the airline, is 767-346 JA8266.

Left:
Although one of Boeing's largest customers, Japan Airlines has been operating McDonnell Douglas DC-10s since 1976. To replace them ten MD-11s are being acquired; deliveries of these are almost complete. These aircraft are known in JAL service as 'J-Birds', and each aircraft is named after a bird. At rest on the Kai Tak ramp between flights is MD-11 JA8581 *Fairy Pitta*.

Below:
The bulk of JAL flights through Kai Tak are operated by Boeing 747 Jumbo jets, of which the airline is the largest operator. Photographed in November 1987 at the point of rotation from runway 31 is JAL's first ever Jumbo, JA8101. This aircraft is a 747-146, the thirty-first 747 built, delivered to the airline in March 1970.

One of the favourite destinations for young Japanese couples on honeymoon is Hawaii. Due to its popularity Japan Airlines has a number of daily flights to Honolulu, many of which are flown in specially painted aircraft. The appearance of such a machine in Hong Kong is rare indeed, and when gaily painted 'Super Resort Express' Boeing 747-246B JA8141 appeared at Kai Tak on 24 September 1995 it certainly aroused excitement among the local enthusiasts.

Left:
The majority of JAL's Jumbo flights into Kai Tak are operated by the newer -400 variant like JA8911.

Below:
To enable Japan Airlines to serve Taipei without incurring the wrath of the Communist Chinese authorities in Beijing the airline set up a subsidiary in 1975 named Japan Asia Airways. A number of these flights routed through Kai Tak, operated by aircraft handed down from the parent carrier. The first equipment comprised the DC-8-61, with JA8050 illustrated. Note the only difference in the livery is the tail logo.

To supplement the DC-8s Japan Asia soon received a few DC-10s from JAL, including DC-10-40 JA8532 seen on take-off on runway 13 in August 1987.

Left:
Japan Asia's fleet has grown with the acquisition of four 747s from JAL, though a similar number of DC-10s are still in use. These now appear in the revised JAL scheme, again the tail logo and titling being the only difference. DC-10-40 JA8531 was photographed about to land on runway 13 on a sunny November afternoon in 1994.

Below:
Japan Airlines operates a sizeable fleet of 747 freighters. To transfer an aircraft to subsidiary Japan Asia is really quite easy: simply remove the letter 'L' from the nose titles and, hey presto, you have Japan Asia! Photographed on 1 October 1995 Boeing 747-246F(SCD) JA8123 taxies on to the runway with a Korean Cargo example awaiting its turn.

Garuda Indonesia operates to Hong Kong from both Jakarta and Denpasar/Bali. During the 1980s the Jakarta flights were almost always operated with 747 equipment, like 747-2U3B PK-GSD *City of Surabaya*. This shot was taken in April 1986 and on the rear fuselage the aircraft wears 'Indonesia Air Show 86' titles, being the official carrier for the first ever such event.

In 1987 Garuda unveiled a new livery comprising a white fuselage and dark blue tail, the latter featuring a stylised turquoise Garuda bird. The airline's 747s are seldom seen at Kai Tak, services now being operated by a mixture of A300, DC-10 and MD-11 equipment. Displaying the current livery is DC-10-30 PK-GIC.

Over the last five years Malaysia Airlines has experienced phenomenal growth and now has one of the largest 737 fleets in Asia. These 737s have only been regular visitors at Kai Tak since 1994, operating a thrice-weekly service from Kuching. Positioned for a perfect landing is 737-4H6 9M-MQF.

Until 1995 Malaysia Airlines flights from Kuala Lumpur were operated by a mixture of Airbus A300s and McDonnell Douglas DC-10s. Nowadays these are operated by newcomers to the inventory, the A330 and (leased) MD-11s, supplemented by Boeing 747s. Banking tightly on to final approach wearing the 1980s livery is DC-10-30 PK-GIB, an aircraft on lease from Garuda.

To encourage tourism many Asian countries have developed programmes titled 'Visit . . .'. Like Korea, Malaysia developed such a scheme for 1994. All aircraft in the Malaysia Airlines inventory wore prominent 'Visit Malaysia 94' stickers on the fuselage, as seen on Boeing 747-4H6 9M-MPD in the airline's current attractive livery.

Hugely successful Singapore Airlines operates a number of 747 freighters; to supplement these a Boeing 737-300 was acquired in 1992 and converted into a freighter for use on regional routes. This aircraft, 9M-SQZ, was a regular into Kai Tak during 1994, departing at 0830 every morning. It is seen at the commencement of its take-off run on the early-morning schedule. Note the close proximity of the buildings to the runway.

From its early success with the 747 it was only a matter of time before Singapore Airlines progressed from the early -200 variants. The stretched upper deck -300 variant was a natural progression, and the first of fourteen of the type, dubbed 'Big Top' by the company, was delivered in April 1983. Taxying to its gate on an uncharacteristically clear day is 747-312 N123KJ.

Following on from the -300 Jumbo comes the -400, and it was no surprise when Singapore Airlines announced large orders for this variant which it has dubbed 'Megatop'. The airline has also taken delivery of the -400F freighter variant, and these are known as 'Mega Ark'. Singapore Airlines has the distinction of operating the 1,000th Boeing 747 built. The aircraft in question, 9V-SMU, was photographed during a visit to Kai Tak on 24 September 1995.

Right:
In the space of a decade Royal Brunei Airlines' services to Hong Kong from Bandar Seri Begawan have progressed from Boeing 737s through the 757 to the 767. The airline was one of the first Asian customers for the 757, the first being delivered at the Indonesia Air Show in 1986. The airline's second of the type, V8-RBB, was photographed soon after delivery in December 1986.

Below:
Another early Asian customer for the 757 was Royal Nepal Airlines. Two of the type were acquired, the second being a Combi variant. These aircraft replaced a pair of Boeing 727s which had previously been used on the Kathmandu run. The airline's simple but pleasing livery is shown to good effect on Boeing 757 9N-ACB against the clear blue skies.

One of the most recent carriers to serve Hong Kong is Myanmar Airways International. The airline was only formed in 1993, initially utilising a leased Boeing 757 from Royal Brunei. It has since replaced this with a Boeing 737-400 leased from Malaysia Airlines. The aircraft in question, 9M-MMH, is seen taxying for departure to Yangon (formerly Rangoon) in November 1994.

Air Lanka has operated Lockheed TriStars on its Colombo–Hong Kong service for many years. In 1994, however, the airline received the first of three Airbus A340s on order, and the type was quickly put to use on this lucrative route. Photographed only a matter of weeks after delivery is the airline's second A340-300 4R-ADB.

Biman Bangladesh Airlines currently operates DC-10s on its Dacca–Hong Kong route. It was not always so, as during the 1980s and early 1990s the Boeing 707 was the favoured type on the route. The airline was probably the last to use this famous Boeing jetliner on scheduled passenger services to Kai Tak. With a typical Hong Kong backdrop Boeing 707 S2-ACE rests on what at the time was the long-term park, used for aircraft either night stopping or spending the day prior to an evening departure.

Air India introduced its newly delivered Airbus A310s to Hong Kong towards the end of 1986. These twin-jets are supplemented by the carrier's ageing 747 Jumbos on flights from Bombay via Delhi. Flights operated by 747s continue on to Tokyo. Poised for touchdown on runway 13 is A310-300 VT-EJJ.

Banking to align with runway 13 over the
rooftops of some of Kowloon's older buildings
is an Air India Boeing 747-237B.

American and Antipodean Visitors

A considerable number of American tourists visit Hong Kong every year yet, when compared to the airports of many European cities, the number of services by US airlines is rather low. Northwest Airlines, for example, has a major hub at Tokyo, yet the carrier has just one service a day into Kai Tak. United Airlines has the largest presence of any US carrier, thanks to its 1987 purchase of Pan American's trans-Pacific routes and the aircraft to operate them. Continental Micronesia links Hong Kong with the South Pacific islands using Boeing 727s, while Delta's Los Angeles service was short-lived and terminated at the end of 1995.

Where US carriers are strong is in the thriving cargo market. An increasing number of 747 freighters use the airport, and FedEx has recently opened an Asian hub at the former US naval base at Cubi Point in the Philippines. Canadian Pacific has served Hong Kong for many years, first with DC-8s and later DC-10s. A merger with Pacific Western resulted in Canadian Airlines International, which has since increased capacity by using Boeing 747-400s. In 1995 Air Canada was finally permitted to compete with its rival, and also uses the 747-400. Air New Zealand serves Auckland twice-weekly using Boeing 747-200s with a very high standard of in-flight service. The Australian national carrier, Qantas, has operated into Kai Tak for many years. It currently operates a daily 747-400 service to Sydney as well as direct flights to Brisbane and Cairns with 767s . With an Asian hub at Singapore at least four Qantas 767s a day can be seen in Kai Tak. Newcomer on the Sydney route is Ansett Australia Airlines, now operating five times weekly to Sydney using leased Boeing 747-300s. The only South American airline operating into Kai Tak is Brazilian carrier Varig which operates MD-11s to Rio de Janeiro and São Paulo.

Continental Micronesia is a subsidiary of Continental Airlines and, as the name suggests, serves the islands of Micronesia. The airline has bases in Honolulu and Guam, the latter being the base for its fleet of Boeing 727s which serve the islands in this idyllic part of the world. The airline serves Guam and Saipan four times weekly from Kai Tak using Boeing 727s like N296AS.

Delta Air Lines was a late entrant to the Hong Kong scene serving Los Angeles direct with MD-11 tri-jets. The service, however, did not meet the airline's expectations, and it pulled off the route towards the end of 1995, reassigning the aircraft to the Atlanta–London/Gatwick route. This was perhaps due to the distance involved, being at the extreme limit of the MD-11's range. In contrast, United Airlines and Cathay Pacific both use Boeing 747-400 aircraft on this route. Captured about to rotate on take-off from runway 13 is Delta MD-11 N804DE.

So buoyant is cargo traffic out of Hong Kong that from the US more cargo operators than scheduled airlines fly to the territory. Of these FedEx – previously known as Federal Express – has by far been serving Hong Kong the longest. The carrier's DC-10s are no longer seen at Kai Tak, having been replaced by the ever increasing fleet of MD-11Fs. Illustrated in November 1994 on the first ever visit to Hong Kong displaying the new FedEx livery is MD-11F N601FE.

Right:
Supplementing the MD-11s, FedEx Jumbos are still a regular sight at Kai Tak. Boeing 747-249F(SCD) N631FE sports the old Federal Express livery and titles. This aircraft has been a regular at Kai Tak for many years, though a number of those appearances were in the guise of N806FT of Flying Tigers.

Below:
The name Flying Tigers is up there with Pan American when one talks of US aviation legends. This once great, well-known freight operator is no more, having been swallowed up by Federal Express in 1989. In happier times, 747 freighter N817FT makes an approach to runway 13 in January 1988. This aircraft now serves with United Parcel Service.

Another well-known name in US freight circles is Connie Kalitta, a Detroit–Willow Run-based operator with a sizeable DC-8 fleet. In recent years the airline has changed its name to Kalitta American International Airways, and has added several 747 freighters, like N706CK, to its inventory.

Among its sizeable 747 fleet Northwest Airlines operates seven freighter Jumbos. During the 1980s these aircraft were easily identifiable thanks to the highly polished natural metal fuselage. Photographed in January 1987 when the airline was still known as Northwest Orient Airlines is Boeing 747-251F(SCD) N617US.

Aircraft on the ground do not make money, therefore turn-rounds have to be as quick as possible. This means that during this phase there is a constant hustle and bustle of men and machines swarming round the aircraft. This is evident here as a pair of Northwest Cargo 747s are being loaded at HACTL–Hong Kong Air Cargo Terminal.

Above:
Sharing the long-term park with a United 747 in October 1987 is elderly Northwest Orient Boeing 747-151 N609US. To mark route expansion eastwards to Europe the airline has since dropped the Orient part of its name. Northwest has since taken delivery of ten longer range series -400 Jumbos and, although these were used on the Seattle route for a short time, the airline has reverted to the older -200 variant on the route.

Left:
Founded as recently as 1993 New York-based Polar Air Cargo is a fast-expanding 747-equipped freight operator. Usually at least one of the airline's aircraft can be seen at Kai Tak, though I have seen as many as three at a time. With barely 1,000 feet of runway remaining the nosewheel of heavily laden 747 N855FT is just inches off the concrete at the start of a long trans-Pacific flight.

A variant now seldom seen at Kai Tak, the
Boeing 747SP. During the 1980s both South
African Airways and United Airlines operated
this 'baby Jumbo' into the territory's airport.
United's activities at Kai Tak increased signifi-
cantly with the acquisition of Pan American's
trans-Pacific routes and a number of aircraft,
including the SP and L-1011. Captured on film
in December 1987 newly painted in United
livery is 747SP N141UA.

During the 1980s the DC-10 operated the bulk of United flights into Hong Kong, including aircraft leased from Canadian Pacific. Now virtually all flights are undertaken by the Boeing 747-400. The approach to Kai Tak's runway 13 is without doubt one of the most difficult in the world, and it's not surprising that from time to time someone just doesn't get it quite right. One such occasion was this approach by United 747-422 N191UA in November 1994. Compare the aircraft's position relative to checkerboard hill – and he's definitely low on the approach and banking tightly to align correctly with the runway.

A few seconds later and the pilot has made an excellent recovery, poised for a perfect landing.

The Boeing 747 freighter is the favoured type of most cargo operators into Kai Tak, the world's 747 freighter hub. United Parcel Service is one of the most recent exponents of the type, which has allowed it to extend its wide-ranging US network westwards. The aircraft featured here, Boeing 747-121F(SCD) N682UP, has been seen elsewhere in this book when serving with Flying Tigers as N817FT. This aircraft started its life with Pan American as N654PA.

One of the longest-serving overseas airlines into Hong Kong was Canadian Pacific. In 1987 a merger with Pacific Western resulted in a name change to Canadian Airlines International, and a new livery. Wearing the current livery lined up for departure from runway 13 is DC-10-30 C-GCPG. Note the control tower in the background; the brown building to the left is the airport hotel. On the top floor of this building is 'The Flying Machine Bar', from where panoramic views of the ramp can be enjoyed over an expensive cool beer.

Canadian Airlines International flights from Vancouver are now operated almost exclusively by its fleet of four Boeing 747-475 aircraft. The first of these, C-GMWW *Maxwell W. Ward,* was delivered in December 1990 and is seen seconds from touchdown. The airline's main competitor Air Canada received approval to operate to Kai Tak in 1995.

Right:
The sole South American airline to operate to Kai Tak is the Brazilian carrier Varig. It operates twice-weekly MD-11 flights to Rio de Janeiro, albeit with three intermediate stops. Taxying for departure is MD-11 PP-VPL.

Below:
Air New Zealand's 747s have been a regular sight at Kai Tak for many years, and the airline currently operates a twice-weekly service to Auckland using its Boeing 747-200s, leaving the -400 variants to operate the long-haul sectors to Europe. Seen on final approach in October 1995 is 747-219B ZK-NZZ *Tokomaru,* an aircraft which was delivered in 1982.

Qantas Boeing 747s have been a regular sight at Kai Tak for many a year, from the series -200 to the -300 and, currently, the -400. The airline's kangaroo logo on a bright red tail stands out well in the afternoon sunshine as Boeing 747-338 VH-EBT *City of Wagga Wagga* taxies to its gate in this July 1986 shot.

Qantas now operates so many flights to Asia
that the airline operates a hub from
Singapore's Changi Airport where a number
of the company's Boeing 767s are based. Kai
Tak usually receives four Qantas 767s a day,
one at midday and then a convoy of three at
dusk. Lined up for take-off on runway 13
is Boeing 767-338ER VH-OGH *City of
Parramatta*.

Relative newcomer to the Hong Kong scene is Ansett Australia Airlines. Having finally received authorisation to compete with state carrier Qantas the airline has leased three Boeing 747-300s to serve Osaka–Kansai and Hong Kong. Services commenced in 1994, and the airline has an agreement with Virgin Atlantic for onward transfer of connecting passengers. Photographed in October 1995 wearing Ansett's current tail logo is Boeing 747-300 VH-INJ.

Air Nauru operated a twice-weekly Boeing 737 service from its island home of the same name. Recently, however, the service has been discontinued, despite the airline upgrading to Boeing 737-400 equipment in 1993. Photographed on the runway at Kai Tak in December 1987 is Boeing 737-2L7 C2-RN6.

Europe and Elsewhere

With the cost of air travel falling considerably in real terms, long-haul travel is becoming more accessible all the time. More and more Europeans are taking advantage of this, forsaking the beaches of Benidorm and Biarritz to sample the different cultures of places like Bangkok, Bali or Hong Kong. Yet surprisingly, on Europe to Hong Kong routes the increase in the number of seats available is on the low side. There has been a slight increase in frequency on some routes, and the last few years has seen new services introduced by Virgin Atlantic and Aeroflot. However, Alitalia and Swissair, for example, have reduced the number of seats available by switching from 747 to MD-11 equipment. The sole African carrier serving Hong Kong is South African Airways, while from the Middle East Gulf Air now has competition from Emirates.

From BOAC and its Boeing 707s and VC-10s to British Airways and its Super VC-10s and Boeing 747s, the British state airline has always had a strong presence at Kai Tak, as is fitting with the last outpost of the Empire. In the 1980s British Airways 747s competed head to head with British Caledonian on the London/Gatwick–Hong Kong route. The independent airline had a large share of the market, thanks to its superior standard of service and friendly crews. Sadly for the British aviation industry British Caledonian, its aircraft and routes were taken over by British Airways, which suddenly had two daily Gatwick-bound flights. The airline currently operates the -400 series Jumbo on the route, though in 1986 it was the -200s which carried out the work. Illustrated decelerating after landing on runway 31 is 747-236B G-BDXA *City of Cardiff.*

Like a number of carriers British Airways has formed a subsidiary company to operate services to Taiwan and avoid re-criminations from the People's Republic of China. This is known as British Asia Airways and was founded in 1993. The airline's livery is identical to that of BA, with the exception of the tail logo. The thrice-weekly London/Heathrow–Taipei service routes via Hong Kong, giving enthusiasts the opportunity to photograph Boeing 747-436 G-BNLZ *City of Perth*.

British Caledonian Airlines initially operated DC-10s on its London/Gatwick–Hong Kong route, though in 1987 the carrier's Boeing 747s took over the task. When BCAL's fleet was subsumed into that of British Airways the 747s served for only a short time as they were incompatible with the rest of the BA Jumbo fleet. Although BA did not want the DC-10s it soon found out that it had inherited an excellent aircraft; indeed the aircraft in question are still providing sterling service. With the Lion Rampant adorning the tail, appropriately registered DC-10-30 G-DC10 named *Flora McDonald–The Scottish Heroine* flares for touchdown on runway 13.

Latest British entrant on the London–Hong Kong route is Richard Branson's Virgin Atlantic Airways. Having flown with the airline on the route twice recently I can vouch for the impressive standard of service and in-flight entertainment which is certainly superior to that of the other two airlines on the route. Virgin uses its brand-new Airbus A340-300s on the route, flying non-stop in around thirteen hours, depending on the winds, and using a lot less fuel than the Boeing 747-400. Note the flexing of the long wings on A340-300 G-VBUS *Lady in Red* as it is caught on approach to runway 13 in the early-evening sunshine.

Air France continues to serve Paris–Charles
de Gaulle Airport with a daily Boeing 747-400
service. Photographed on short finals still
rather high and in the bank is 747-428(SCD)
F-GISC. This aircraft is minus the red tail
stripe of the normal Air France livery, the
reason being that it had previously been operated by subsidiary Air France Asie on
services to Taiwan.

Another European carrier operating 747-400 equipment from its capital to Hong Kong is KLM–Royal Dutch Airlines. The airline has a fleet of sixteen series -400s, all of which are named after destinations served by the type. Seen banking on to final approach is 747-406(SCD) PH-BFH which, rather appropriately, is named *City of Hong Kong*.

Dutch charter operator Martinair has been
flying to Hong Kong for many years now,
using both DC-10s and Boeing 747s in the last
decade. The airline operates both passenger
and cargo charters to the territory, so aircraft
like Boeing 747-21AC(SCD) PH-MCE prove
ideal for the service.

Right:
A few seconds from touchdown Lufthansa Boeing 747-230B D-ABZH looks immaculate in the late-afternoon sunshine. The carrier's old livery dates this shot to April 1987.

Below:
The first time you see an aircraft the size of a Jumbo banking over the Kowloon rooftops on to final approach for runway 13 you think 'Wow!' However, after a while it all becomes rather run-of-the-mill and you think nothing of it. Every once in a while, though, you get one aircraft whose approach makes those who witness it gaze in awe or mutter the odd expletive, this was the sight of Lufthansa Boeing 747-430(SCD) D-ABTH *Duisburg* cranking round in a fighter-type turn on 11 November 1994.

Left:
Alitalia Boeing 747-243B(SCD) I-DEMF photographed at the end of a flight from Rome in August 1987. In common with many carriers serving Hong Kong a Combi variant with a side cargo door is operated on services to the territory, maximising yield with a mix of passengers and freight.

Below:
Alitalia now uses MD-11s on its Rome service, and the airline's pilots can be guaranteed to fly some of the most 'interesting' approaches to runway 13. Showing off the graceful lines of the McDonnell Douglas tri-jet to good effect is I-DUPI *Giacomo Puccini*, a Combi variant.

The pilot of this Alitalia MD-11 misjudged this approach somewhat! He is well below the glidepath and about to disappear from view. Thankfully he managed to gain height, though still landed in the sterile area of runway 13 which should only be used for aircraft at the start of their take-off roll.

SAS–Scandinavian Airlines uses Boeing 767-300ER aircraft on its four-times-weekly service from Copenhagen, which by at least one hour is the shortest flight from Western Europe to Hong Kong. The airline has a fleet of fifteen 767s which are in four different configurations, including some in a polar fit which carry additional survival equipment on services to Greenland and over the Arctic to Seattle. Photographed passing Lion Rock while operating flight SK991 is SE-DOC *Gudrun Viking.*

Swissair uses predominantly MD-11 equipment on its five-times-a-week service from Zurich, some of which route via Geneva. In mid-1994 the airline introduced a new livery which omits the once familiar cheatline. One of the first aircraft to appear in the new scheme was MD-11 HB-IWN, seen here a matter of weeks after delivery in November 1994. This aircraft now wears Swissair Asia titles, this subsidiary being formed to operate a Taipei service.

One of the most recent European airlines to commence Hong Kong services is Aeroflot Russian International Airlines. The airline achieved notoriety on 23 March 1994 when an A310 bound for Hong Kong from Moscow crashed in Siberia with no survivors. Having examined tape transcripts and the aircraft's black box it transpired that the aircraft captain let his fifteen-year-old son take control while both pilots were off the flight deck. The youth apparently disconnected the autopilot and the aircraft went out of control. Featured is leased Airbus A310-300 F-OGQR *Rachmaninov*, sister ship of the aircraft which crashed.

Sole African carrier operating into Kai Tak is South African Airways. The airline's Jumbos have been plying the route from Johannesburg for many years, initially with the SP variant, and currently with the -200 and -300 series. Illustrated a few seconds from touchdown on runway 13 is 747-344 ZS-SAU *Kapstad*. The airline uses Afrikaans titling and names on the starboard side and English on the port.

Two Middle East carriers serve Hong Kong, the most recent being Dubai-based Emirates which uses both the A310 and A300. One of the latter, A6-EKM, an A300-600R, is seen here on final approach in the weak late-afternoon sunshine.

The first Middle East-based operator to fly to Hong Kong was Gulf Air using Lockheed TriStars, with A40-TV seen here about to park at Gate 1.

Against a background of prominent tower blocks and an even more prominent hillside is Gulf Air Boeing 767-3P6ER A40-GV *Dukhan*. The 767 now operates all the airline's services from Abu Dhabi and Bahrain, having replaced the TriStars.

Light and Rotary Selection

This section deals with the military scene in Hong Kong and some of the light aircraft based in the territory. The British military base is at Sek Kong in the New Territories; their helicopters are frequently seen in and around Kai Tak. The simple but rugged Westland Scout AH1 has served the Army Air Corps well in Hong Kong. Operated by 660 Squadron, the helicopters fly in support of British forces based in the territory as well as in support of the civilian police. In the latter role they were kept fairly busy during the 1980s deterring and helping to capture illegal immigrants crossing the Chinese border seeking their fortune in Hong Kong. No.660 Squadron disbanded on 31 December 1993 as part of the run-down of British forces prior to the handover of the territory to China. Also Sek Kong-based and with a similar role to 660 Squadron is No.28 Squadron Royal Air Force with a fleet of Westland Wessex HC2 helicopters. This unit is still extant, though its fleet has been reduced in numbers in recent years.

Based at Kai Tak, the Royal Hong Kong Auxiliary Air Force (RHKAAF) operated a fixed-wing and helicopter fleet. To reflect more its role of supporting the police and other authorities the RHKAAF has since changed its name to the Government Flying Service (GFS). It has also disposed of most of its fixed-wing assets, retaining just a Beech 200 and a BN-2 Islander. The ever-increasing rotary fleet is based around the S-76 helicopter.

There are only a few privately owned light aircraft based in the territory, though the Hong Kong Aviation Club (HKAC) has a small band of enthusiastic members. Due to the increasing number of movements at Kai Tak these light aircraft are being squeezed out, and the HKAC now bases most of its fleet at Sek Kong. Most flights between the two airports have to be undertaken early in the morning.

Photographed over the eastern end of Hong Kong Island in January 1988 is 660 Squadron Scout AH1 XW797 'G'. Just visible in front of the nose is the threshold of runway 31 extending into Victoria Harbour.

In this book the imposing Lion Rock appears in the background of many shots. This is a view of the prominent feature from the northern side. No.28 Squadron Wessex HC2 XT675 'J' passes abeam the rock inbound to Kai Tak which is visible in the background. The most direct route between Sek Kong and Kai Tak is about an eight-minute flight, a journey which by road can take anywhere from forty-five to ninety minutes depending on traffic.

Left:
All of 28 Squadron's Wessexes are finished in this camouflaged scheme offset by high visibility white stripes. Photographed over the town of Yuen Long in the New Territories inbound to Sek Kong is Wessex HC2 XT605 'E'.

Below:
During the 1980s the RHKAAF's rotary fleet comprised three Aérospatiale SA365 Dauphin helicopters which replaced the Alouette III. These have since been replaced by Sikorsky S-76s.

Right:
For primary training the RHKAAF utilised a pair of Scottish Aviation Bulldogs, which were eventually replaced by the Slingsby T67, the first of which arrived in 1987. The Bulldogs were eventually sold to the UK where they were rather appropriately registered G-HONG and G-KONG!

Below:
Towards the end of 1987 the RHKAAF acquired a Beech 200 Super King Air to replace a Cessna 404 Titan. The Beech is used for surveillance of Hong Kong waters and for search and rescue purposes over the expanse of the South China Sea around the territory. The aircraft in question, HKG-8, is seen here on the runway at Sek Kong during a crew training sortie in January 1988.

Sleek-looking and in the smart GFS livery is S-76 VR-HZH. With the change from Auxiliary Air Force status to Government Flying Service the aircraft went on to the civil register. To cater for airport expansion the GFS had to vacate its hangar which was demolished to make way for additional ramp space. A new hangar and other facilities have been built adjacent to the new ramp, which has a splendid view looking across Victoria Harbour to Hong Kong Island. (*Phil Parker*)

Privately owned and appropriately registered Cessna 172RG VR-HRG, the letters RG standing for retractable gear. The aircraft was photographed in June 1987 flying along the waterfront of Hong Kong Island. The building with the twin glass towers with red trim is the Hong Kong–Macau ferry terminal.

Left:
In late 1986 a group of seven pilots, whose numbers included two from Cathay Pacific, formed a syndicate and purchased a Cap 10. This fully aerobatic aircraft was allocated the registration VR-HUC, and from then on was known to everyone as 'Uncle Charlie'. This photograph of the aircraft was taken over Plover Cove in January 1987.

Below:
'Uncle Charlie' heads for home into the setting sun.

The HKAC have a single Cessna 182, VR-HHF. The aircraft is used predominantly by the parachute club at Sek Kong where it is based.

In 1987 the oil company Caltex promoted a
flying scholarship scheme which involved
one of the HKAC aircraft being painted in
Caltex house colours. The aircraft in question,
Cessna 152 VR-HHN, was photographed on
14 June 1987, a few days after the aircraft was
sprayed in the Caltex scheme.

An aerial shot of the Kai Tak ramp in July 1986. Just out of the picture lower left is the long-term park, while the two buildings on the upper left of the picture are the fire station and RHKAAF complex. Both of these have since been demolished to make way for additional ramp space.

The same area as it looks today. To the lower right of the long-term park an additional area of ramp has been laid on land once used by the Hong Kong Police. (*Phil Parker*)

Right:
Right:
Taken in July 1986 this shot looks towards the terminal from runway 31 and the adjacent parallel taxiway. The area on the upper right where the boats are anchored was the infamous rather noxious, 'nullah'. The area has since been filled in and is now additional ramp space.

Below:
Parked on gates 1 and 2 are a Cathay Pacific TriStar and Northwest Orient Boeing 747. The 'Orient' part of the title indicates the shot was taken in 1987, as the airline is now simply Northwest Airlines.

Is it a bird, a plane, superman? It is in fact the navigation and anti-collision lights of an aircraft about to land on runway 13 at dusk in November 1994. Using a slow shutter speed the aircraft type is unidentifiable. What is identifiable, peeking above the Kowloon buildings, is Victoria Peak on Hong Kong Island.

A similar shot some thirty minutes later shows another set of lights from another aircraft about to touch down on runway 13. The lights of the numerous buildings on the background are on Hong Kong Island across Victoria Harbour.

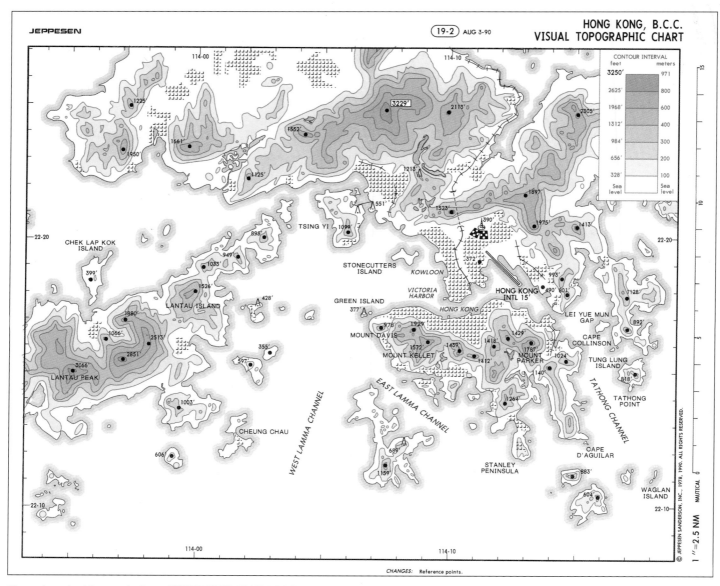